A GIFT FOR

Joanne W.

FROM

Kayla 12/07

Soul Food: Wisdom & Inspiration to Feed Your Spirit
Copyright © 2007 by Hallmark Licensing, Inc.

Published by Hallmark Books,
a division of Hallmark Cards, Inc.,
Kansas City, MO 64141
Visit us on the web at www.Hallmark.com.

Art Director: Kevin Swanson
Editorial Director: Todd Hafer

Editorial development by Scott Degelman & Associates,
with additional writing by Trieste Van Wyngarden

Designer: Craig Bissell
Production Artist: Dan Horton

Printed and bound in China
ISBN: 978-1-59530-164-2

First Edition, September 2007
10 9 8 7 6 5 4 3 2 1

BOK5517

Soul Food

WISDOM AND INSPIRATION
TO FEED YOUR SPIRIT

GIFT BOOKS
from Hallmark

Hungry?

THERE IS CERTAINLY NO shortage of things to eat in this world. Fresh fruit and veggies. Steak and mashed potatoes. Biscuits and gravy. All kinds of good stuff to fill your stomach.

Or, you can fill your brain with nonstop music, thrilling action shows, and every sort of visual distraction you can name. Everyone with any kind of appetite can find something to fill up on. Of course, hunger – for the entertaining or the edible – comes back pretty quickly, but, hey, that's life.

Or is it? Not according to God. He promises something better. "*Come to me,*" he says. "*Let me carry those burdens for a while. Let me rub your tired feet, sort out the confusion, feed your spirit.*" And what God feeds us keeps us full – full of joy, full of hope. God's food is, truly, soul food. It does much more than titillate the senses. And, although it doesn't come in a wrapper, if it had a nutrition label, we'd see that it offers us 100% of our daily allowance of everything we need to thrive – and then some.

That's what this book is all about. Soul food. The healthy, delicious, funny, smart, encouraging stuff that feeds us from the inside out. So sit down and take a big, juicy bite of God's love, wisdom, and inspiration. There's always enough to go around!

A Childlike Faith

$\mathcal{E}$VER WONDER what childlike faith really looks like? Here's your chance to hear it – from the experts. Kids have intriguing and wonderful ideas about who God is. We asked kids from across the nation questions about God, heaven, Jesus, and life in general. You might be surprised at the answers. You might be amused. You might even gain an insight or two. After all, God works in mysterious ways.

WHAT IS HEAVEN LIKE?

"It's blue like the sky and all the
food tastes good. And you can make
the weather anything you want."

BRYCE, AGE 7

"It's way up in the sky,
and Harry Potter's there."

COREY, AGE 3

"It's very big, and it's not scary."

CARRIE, AGE 3

"It's a cool place
where everything
goes right."

BRENNAN, AGE 9

"It's cool, and you can skateboard
there without getting hurt."

CHARLES, AGE 11

"It's where you see all the people
you miss."

MICHAEL, AGE 14

"It's surrounded by pearly gates.
The streets are made of gold.
The sky there is a beautiful misty blue,
and the air is clean."

LILY, AGE 9

"Like the coolest museum that doesn't
cost anything – and you never
have to go home."

NICK, AGE 13

"Heaven is like earth, only with angels."

TYLER, AGE 8

"Heaven is like the best
amusement park ever!"

JESSIE, AGE 6

"Heaven is where I'll see my mom again."

A.J., AGE 13

How does a person get into Heaven?

"You ask Jesus in your heart – which I've done numerous times by now."

BRENNAN, AGE 9

"Believe in Jesus."

BRYCE, AGE 7

"Well, don't kill anybody; that's for sure."

CHARLES, AGE 11

"I think you have to take, like, a long trip."

JESSIE, AGE 6

"Chee-suss!"

CARRIE, AGE 3

"Don't get too mad
when your parents
tell you to clean up
your room."

Tony, 13

"Ask forgiveness for the sins you've done."

MICHAEL, 14

"Help someone else to get to know God."

BRANDON, 14

"Have Jesus in your heart."

JOSH, 12

"You stay in heaven by never
leaving heaven."

LAUREL, 3

"Do good in the subjects in school – even the ones that you don't really like."

ANDREW, 8

"Eat all your vegetables."

TYLER, 9

"Feed the poor and heal the sick."

ALEX, 11

"Live for God."

NICK, 12

"If you become really cool friends with Jesus, He will take you all the cool places He goes, like heaven."

JACOB, 14

HOW WERE PEOPLE CREATED?

"God used dirt. Lots of dirt to make boys."

JESSIE, 6

"God used magic."

CARRIE, 3

"God did it – in, like,
7 days or something."

SAM, 7

"It's a mystery – kind of like
'Where do babies come from?'"

FRANCINE, 8

"I don't know how they were created,
but I know why: To be God's friends."

BRYCE, 7

WHAT'S THE BEST THING GOD EVER MADE?

"Me."

JESSIE, 6

"My mommy."

CARRIE, 3

"Video Games – and I realize He didn't actually make them. But, He made people and THEY did."

BRENNAN, 9

"Harry Potter."

COREY, 3

"Happiness –
which you get when
you trust God."

MARISSA, 12

"Well, my dog would have to be
right up there."

KYLIE, 10

"Families!"

JAY, 11

"Love."

LILY, 9

WHAT DO YOU LOVE ABOUT GOD?

"He helps me be calm when I'm scared."

HARRY, 6

"He's always there,
even when I forget that he is."

JOSEPHINE, 8

"I like that he's the enemy of that little
red dude with the pitchfork."

LILY, 9

"He can hear, like, a gazillion prayers
at one time."

RYAN, 9

"He's the one person
who's never too busy for me."

RORY, 13

"He's Jesus' daddy."

SOLOMON, 5

"He understands me."

JENNY, 13

WHAT WILL YOU LIKE MOST ABOUT HEAVEN?

"I'll see my uncle and great-grandmother again, and they won't treat me like a little kid because we'll all be the same age."

MICHAEL, 12

"There will be lot less crime than there is down here."

JAMES, 11

"In heaven, you can play hacky-sack and keep it in the air for five hours."

DARREN, 10

"Heaven will feel
like the most
comfortable bed in
the world – even
when you're
standing up."

BRANDON, 13

"Everybody will get along in heaven.
No fighting or arguing.
Everybody is laughing."

MICHAEL, 14

"Hacky-sack will be banned
because it's stupid, and God doesn't
allow stupid things."

NICK, 14

"In heaven, you'll get gold pipes
on your skateboard."

JAMES, 11

"I'll be an awesome singer up there."

TIM, 13

"You can squirt ketchup on people's shirts
and it won't leave a stain."

ANDREW, 12

"There's a fruit in heaven – half grapefruit,
half orange – that's as soft as a peach
and tastes like magic."

CHRIS, 10

"You get to see God, and
He has a clean face."

A.J., 11

"I can fly in heaven."

DUSTIN, 9

"No more colds!"

GABRIELLE, 8

"There's never-ending food in heaven."

ALLEN, 9

"There are lots of animals in heaven,
but mostly dogs, because all dogs
go to heaven."

ALEX, 12

"All the cars have gold-plated hubcaps."

TONY, 13

"You can do phenomenal
skateboard tricks in heaven."

SCOTT, 13

"You can run in your bare feet
and never get a cut or blister."

ANDREW, 12

"There will be one huge
happy family, and everyone
is always welcome home."

SHERRY, 11

"There are really
cool video games
in heaven."

DOMINICK, 13

WHAT CAN A KID DO TO MAKE GOD SMILE?

"Help as many people as you can."

SCOTT, 13

"Remember to always go potty
in the potty chair."

SALLY, 4

"Do good things, like stay at the table
even when you want to get down
and play with toys."

SOLOMON, 5

"Serve God, which means saying
'Please' and 'Thank you' ...a lot."

C.J., 7

"Be honest – like when it was you
that ate all the Snickers bars."

NICK, 8

"Be like God, forgiving people
and all that stuff."

STEPHEN, 13

"You make God happy by *not* doing all the
things the Bible tells you not to do."

CARMEN, 12

"Love people as much as God loves them."

SHERRY, 12

100 Favorite
Bible Verses

*D*O YOU HAVE A favorite Bible verse – one that challenges you, comforts you, or inspires you – even on the toughest of days? One that stirs your soul, no matter how many times you hear it? Read on, and see if your "life verse" is among the following 100 passages. And if it's not, feel free to write it in!

1.

Cast all your anxiety on him
because he cares for you.

1 Peter 5:7

2.

Let the peace of Christ rule in your hearts,
to which indeed you were called
in the one body.

Colossians 3:15 NRSV

3.

Do not be anxious about anything,
but in everything, by prayer
and petition, with thanksgiving,
present your requests to God.

Philippians 4:6

4.

There is neither
Jew nor Greek,
slave nor free,
male nor female,
for you are all one
in Christ Jesus.

GALATIANS 3:28

5.

God created humankind in his image,
in the image of God he created them;
male and female he created them.

GENESIS 1:27 NRSV

6.

A gentle answer turns away wrath,
but a harsh word stirs up anger.

PROVERBS 15:1

7.

We know that in all things God works for
the good of those who love him, who have
been called according to his purpose.

ROMANS 8:28

8.

The LORD is good,
a refuge in times of trouble.
He cares for those who trust in him....

NAHUM 1:7 TNIV

9.

You will keep in perfect peace him whose
mind is steadfast, because he trusts in you.
Trust in the LORD forever, for the LORD,
the LORD, is the Rock eternal.

ISAIAH 26:3-4

10.

The LORD your God is with you,
the Mighty Warrior who saves.
He will take great delight in you;
in his love he will no longer rebuke you,
but will rejoice over you with singing.

ZEPHANIAH 3:17 TNIV

11.

"For I know the plans I have for you," declares the LORD, "plans to prosper you and not to harm you, plans to give you a hope and a future. Then you will call upon me and come and pray to me, and I will listen to you. You will seek me and find me when you seek me with all your heart."

JEREMIAH 29:11-13

72nd
Drive

DEA # _____

MICHAEL OSTAD, M.D.

2508 OCEAN AVENUE
BROOKLYN, NY 11229
718-258-1800   FAX: 718-743-3944

110-45 QUEENS BOULEVARD
FOREST HILLS, NY 11375
718-575-3500   FAX: 718-575-5095

NY LIC NO. 197422

NAME _____

ADDRESS _____ DATE _____

℞ (Please Print)

10/18   9am

_____ M.D.

THIS PRESCRIPTION WILL BE FILLED GENERICALLY
UNLESS PRESCRIBER WRITES D A W IN THE BOX BELOW

☐ LABEL

REFILL _____ TIMES

☐ PRN   ☐ NR

DISPENSE AS WRITTEN

18-MAY-00

07-100500522-1-17824_0008

12.

So we fix our eyes not on what is seen,
but on what is unseen. For what is seen is
temporary, but what is unseen is eternal.

2 Corinthians 4:18

13.

With all your heart you must trust the
LORD and not your own judgment.
Always let him lead you, and he will
clear the road for you to follow.

Proverbs 3:5-6 CEV

14.

How great is the love the Father has
lavished on us, that we should be called
the children of God! And that is
what we are!

1 John 3:1

15.

God's dwelling place is now among the
people, and he will dwell with them.
They will be his people, and God himself
will be with them and be their God.

REVELATION 21:3 TNIV

16.

Whoever loves money never has money
enough; whoever loves wealth is never
satisfied with his income.

ECCLESIASTES 5:10

17.

The love of money causes all kinds
of trouble.

1 TIMOTHY 6:10 CEV

18.

It is better to have a partner than go it
alone. Share the work, share the wealth.
And if one falls down, the other helps...

ECCLESIASTES 4:9-10 THE MESSAGE

19.

Jesus said: "When you do something
for someone else, don't call attention to
yourself....When you help someone out,
don't think about how it looks.
Just do it – quietly and unobtrusively."

MATTHEW 6:2-4 THE MESSAGE

20.

A friend loves at all times.

PROVERBS 17:17

21.

Some friends play at friendship, but a true
friend sticks closer than one's nearest kin.

PROVERBS 18:24 NRSV

22.

One who is trustworthy in spirit
keeps a confidence.

PROVERBS 11:3 NRSV

23.

Whatever you do, work at it with all
your heart, as working for the Lord,
not for human masters.

COLOSSIANS 3:23 TNIV

24.

Love each other as brothers and sisters and
honor others more than you do yourself.

ROMANS 12:10 CEV

25.

One who gives an honest answer gives
a kiss on the lips.

PROVERBS 24:26 NRSV

26.

Encourage each other every day.

HEBREWS 3:13 NCV

27.

When you talk, do not say harmful things
but say what people need – words that will
help others become stronger.

EPHESIANS 4:29 NCV

28.

What does the LORD require of you?
To act justly and to love mercy and
to walk humbly with your God.

MICAH 6:8

29.

Be still and know that I am God.

Psalm 46:10 KJV

30.

Because of the LORD's great love we are
not consumed, for his compassions never
fail. They are new every morning;
great is your faithfulness....

Psalm 46:10 KJV

31.

Be strong and courageous. Do not be
terrified; do not be discouraged,
for the LORD your God will be with
you wherever you go.

Joshua 1:9

32.

I can do all things through Christ
who strengthens me.

Philippians 4:13 NKJV

33.
His love is the wonder of the world.

Psalm 31:21 THE MESSAGE

34.
May the Lord of peace himself give you
peace at all times and in every way.

2 Thessalonians 3:16 NIV

35.
Give your burdens to the LORD,
and he will take care of you.

Psalm 55:22 NLT

36.
My soul finds rest in God alone...
He alone is my rock and my salvation;
he is my fortress, I will never be shaken.

Psalm 62: 1-2 NIV

37.

The LORD your God will go ahead of you.
He will neither fail you nor forsake you.

DEUTERONOMY 31:6 NLT

38.

With God, all things are possible.

MATTHEW 19:26 KJV

39.

The heavens declare the glory of God;
the skies proclaim the work of his hands.

PSALM 19:1

40.

If we confess our sins, He is faithful and
just to forgive us our sins and cleanse us
from all unrighteousness.

1 JOHN 1:9 NKJV

41.

Let us not become weary in doing good,
for at the proper time we will reap a
harvest if we do not give up.

GALATIANS 6:9

42.

Though a righteous man falls seven times,
he rises up again.

PROVERBS 24:16

43.

Make the most of every opportunity you
have for doing good.

EPHESIANS 5:16 TLB

44.

The LORD doesn't see
things the way you see
them. People judge by
outward appearance,
but the LORD looks
at the heart.

1 Samuel 16:7 NLT

45.

"Do not store up for yourselves treasures on earth, where moth and rust destroy, and where thieves break in and steal."

Matthew 6:19-21

46.

For the LORD comforts his people and will have compassion on his afflicted ones.

Isaiah 49:13

47.

Those who look to him are radiant.

Psalm 34:5

48.

"Therefore do not worry about tomorrow,
for tomorrow will worry about itself.
Each day has enough trouble of its own."

MATTHEW 6:34

49.

"So in everything, do to others what you
would have them do to you, for this sums
up the Law and the Prophets."

MATTHEW 7:12

50.

God blesses those who patiently
endure testing and temptation.

JAMES 1:12 NLT

51.

"Whoever wishes to become great among
you shall be your servant."

MATTHEW 20:26 NASB

52.

Pleasant words are as an honeycomb,
sweet to the soul, and health to the bones.

PROVERBS 16:24 NKJV

53.

Let your heart give you joy in the days
of your youth.

ECCLESIASTES 11:9

54.

Follow the way of love....

1 CORINTHIANS 14:1

55.

There shall not any man be able to stand
before thee all the days of thy life:
as I was with Moses, so I will be with thee:
I will not fail thee, nor forsake thee.

JOSHUA 1:5 KJV

56.

God is faithful, by whom ye were called
unto the fellowship of his Son Jesus Christ
our Lord.

1 CORINTHIANS 1:9 KJV

57.

"Come to me, all you who are weary and
burdened, and I will give you rest."

MATTHEW 11:28

58.

Every good and perfect gift
is from above....

JAMES 1:17

59.

And so we know and rely on the love God
has for us. God is love. Whoever lives in
love lives in God, and God in him.

1 JOHN 4:16

60.

Control your temper, for anger labels you a fool.

ECCLESIASTES 7:9 NLT

61.

For the earth will be filled with the knowl-
edge of the glory of the LORD, as the
waters cover the sea

HABAKKUK 2:14

62.

"Do not fear, for I am with you;
do not be dismayed, for I am your God.
I will strengthen you with my
righteous right hand."

ISAIAH 41:10

63.

You are my hiding place;
you will protect me from trouble
And surround me with songs
of deliverance.

PSALM 32:7

64.

Blessed be the LORD your God who has delighted in you...

1 Kings 10:9 NKJV

65.

Never will I leave you; never will I forsake you.

Hebrews 13:5

66.

The Lord is watching his children, listening to their prayers.

1 Peter 3:12 TLB

67.

Those who hope in the LORD will renew their strength. They will soar on wings like eagles; they will run and not grow weary, they will walk and not be faint.

Isaiah 40:31

68.

My grace is sufficient
for thee: for my strength
is made perfect in
weakness.

2 Corinthians 12:9 KJV

69.

The joy of the LORD is your strength.

NEHEMIAH 8:10 KJV

70.

May the grace of the Lord Jesus Christ, and the love of God, and the fellowship of the Holy Spirit be with you....

2 CORINTHIANS 13:14

71.

"I have come that they may have life, and that they may have it more abundantly."

JOHN 10:10 NKJV

72.

"My sheep recognize my voice, and I know them, and they follow me. I give them eternal life and they shall never perish. No one shall snatch them away from me."

JOHN 10:27-28 TLB

73.

You created my inmost being;
you knit me together in my mother's womb. I praise you because I am fearfully and wonderfully made.

PSALM 139:13-14

74.

And we know that in all things God works for the good of those who love him, who have been called according to His purpose.

ROMANS 8:28

75.

A cheerful heart is good medicine.

PROVERBS 17:22

76.

"Where your treasure is,
there your heart will be also."

MATTHEW 6:21

77.

Be joyful in hope, patient in affliction,
faithful in prayer.

ROMANS 12:12

78.

Thy word is a lamp unto my feet, and a
light unto my path.

PSALM 119:105 KJV

79.

Love the LORD your God with all
your heart and with all your soul
and with all your strength.

DEUTERONOMY 6:5

80.

"If you love me, you will obey
what I command."

JOHN 14:15

81.

For the wages of sin is death;
but the gift of God is eternal life
through Jesus Christ our Lord.

ROMANS 6:23

82.

As God's chosen people,
holy and dearly loved, clothe yourselves
with compassion, kindness, humility,
gentleness and patience.

COLOSSIANS 3:12

83.

"What will you gain, if you own the whole
world but destroy yourself? What would
you give to get back your soul?"

MATTHEW 16:26 CEV

84.

The memory of the righteous
will be a blessing....

PROVERBS 10:7

85.

"Be on your guard against all kinds of greed; a man's life does not consist in the abundance of his possessions."

LUKE 12:15

86.

A good name is to be chosen rather
than great riches,
Loving favor rather than silver and gold.

PROVERBS 22:1 NKJV

87.

"Don't let your hearts be troubled.
Trust in God; trust also in me."

JOHN 14:1

88.

So, my dear brothers and sisters,
be strong and immovable. Always work
enthusiastically for the Lord,
for you know that nothing you do
for the Lord is ever useless.

1 CORINTHIANS 15:58 NLT

89.

Be patient with each other,
making allowance for each other's faults
because of your love.

EPHESIANS 4:2 TLB

90.

So now there is no condemnation for
those who belong to Christ Jesus.

ROMANS 9:1 NLT

91.

If you spend yourselves in behalf of
the hungry and satisfy the needs of the
oppressed, then your light will rise in
the darkness, and your night will
become like the noonday.

ISAIAH 58:10

92.

If you are angry,
don't sin by nursing your grudge.

EPHESIANS 4:26 TLB

93.

Live in peace with each other.

1 THESSALONIANS 5:13

94.

"Blessed are the merciful,
for they will be shown mercy."

MATTHEW 5:7

95.

Be kind to one another, tenderhearted,
forgiving one another,
as God in Christ forgave you.

EPHESIANS 4:32 RSV

96.

The Lord is close to the brokenhearted,
and He saves those whose spirits
have been crushed.

PSALM 34:18 NCV

97.

Come back to the Lord your God,
because He is kind and shows mercy.
He doesn't become angry quickly,
and He has great love.

JOEL 2:13 NCV

98.

"Though the mountains be shaken and
the hills be removed, yet my unfailing
love for you will not be shaken...."

Isaiah 54:10

99.

And God shall wipe away all tears from
their eyes; and there shall be no more
death, neither sorrow, nor crying,
neither shall there be any more pain:
for the former things are passed away.

Revelation 21:4 KJV

100.

For God so loved the world,
that he gave his only begotten Son,
that whosoever believeth in him should
not perish, but have everlasting life.

John 3:16 KJV

Faithful Words

$\mathcal{G}$OD HAS PROMISED us that if we ask for his wisdom, he will share it. And sometimes that sharing comes to us via the insights and life experiences of our brothers and sisters in faith. Read on, and be comforted, challenged, and inspired by these classic and contemporary words of wisdom.

God loves you simply because he has
chosen to do so. He loves you when you
don't feel lovely. He loves you when
no one else loves you. God will love
you always. No matter what.

MAX LUCADO

The Lord stands above the new day,
for God has made it. All restlessness,
all impurity, all worry and anxiety
flee before him.

DIETRICH BONHOEFFER

God made you as you are in order
to use you as He planned.

J.C. MACAULEY

Out of difficulties
grow miracles.

JEAN DE LA BRUYERE

Be the living expression of God's kindness:
kindness in your face, kindness in your
eyes, kindness in your smile, kindness in
your warm greeting.

MOTHER TERESA

No problem is so big that it won't fit
in God's hands.

SUZANNE BERRY

God speaks to each of us
in the beauty of every flower,
in the grace of every tree,
in the shimmer of every star.

CAROLYN HOPPE

The greatest gift you can give children is
not your own riches, but revealing
to them their own.

MAX LUCADO

FINDING PEACE

Go to that place today.
You know, that one place where everyone
else just doesn't matter anymore –
the traffic, the deadlines, the stress,
the demands, all the hassles of
doing life in a world like ours.
Go to that quiet place,
It doesn't have to be for long.
Just long enough to breathe,
to be.
Give yourself the gift
of time,
of space,
of solitude.
Go there.
Remember. Listen. Look.
Listen some more.
And in that still, small whisper,
Hear the Lord...
and know you are loved.

SARAH MUELLER

God loves to hear
his children laugh.
What healthy
father doesn't?

MARK LOWRY

God gave my parents lots of patience.
I wish I hadn't used up so much of it.

BEVERLY LAUDIE

Angels can fly because
they take themselves lightly.

G.K. CHESTERTON

It's what you've learned
after you know it all that counts.

JOHN WOODEN

A quiet conscience sleeps in thunder.

ENGLISH PROVERB

All the darkness in the world cannot
extinguish the light of a single candle.

ST. FRANCIS OF ASSISI

The two most powerful warriors are
patience and time.

LEO TOLSTOY

Success is going from failure to failure
without losing your enthusiasm.

ABRAHAM LINCOLN

Genius is eternal patience.

MICHELANGELO

What brings joy to the heart is not so
much the friend's gift as the friend's love.

SAINT AELRED

Every time we encourage others,
we give them a transfusion of courage.

CHARLES SWINDOLL

Sometimes our light goes out but is
nurtured into flame by another
human being. Each of us owes
deepest thanks to those who have
rekindled this light.

ALBERT SCHWEITZER

The most precious gift that one person
can bestow on another is gentle
encouragement.

W. PHILLIP KELLER

Gratitude is the key to happiness.

C.S. LEWIS

Even if the whole world doubts, believe
anyway. With God all things are possible.

PAIGE DERUYSCHER

The better friends you are,
the straighter you can talk.

ST. FRANCIS XAVIER

Friends, if we be honest with ourselves,
we shall be honest with each other.

GEORGE MACDONALD

May the road rise up to meet you.
May the wind be always at your back.
May the sun shine warm on your face;
the rains fall soft upon your fields,
and until we meet again,
May God hold you in the palm
of His hand.

TRADITIONAL GAELIC BLESSING

Beauty comes in all ages, colors, shapes,
and forms. God never makes junk.

KATHY IRELAND

When I stand before God at the end of
my life, I would hope that I would not
have a single bit of talent left
and could say:
"I used everything you gave me."

ERMA BOMBECK

The great thing about getting older is
that you don't lose all the other
ages you've been.

MADELEINE L'ENGLE

Light tomorrow with today.

ELIZABETH BARRETT BROWNING

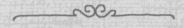

A happy family is
but an earlier heaven.

ANONYMOUS

A baby is God's opinion
that the world should go on.

CARL SANDBURG

I remember my mother's prayers...
and they have clung to me all my life.

ABRAHAM LINCOLN

Honor your father and mother,
even as you honor God, for all three
were partners in your creation.

JEWISH PROVERB

A dad's love waits up when the
rest of the world has already
turned out the lights.

DIANA MANNING

Your children need your presence
more than your presents.

SIR THOMAS MORE

JESSE JACKSON

We are given children to test us
and make us more spiritual.

GEORGE WILL

Whosoever loveth me loveth my hound.

SIR THOMAS MORE

Love begins at home.

MOTHER TERESA

The most important
thing a father can do
for his children is to
love their mother.

REV. THEODORE HESBURGH

That's the beauty of a great friendship –
it makes even the mundane parts
of life colorful.

MELODY CARLSON

Few delights can equal the mere presence
of one whom we trust utterly.

GEORGE MACDONALD

To err is human, to forgive divine.

ALEXANDER POPE

Humanity is never so beautiful as
when praying forgiveness or else
forgiving another.

JEAN PAUL RICHTER

Darkness cannot drive out darkness;
only light can do that. Hate cannot
drive out hate; only love can do that.

MARTIN LUTHER KING JR.

Faith makes all things possible.

D.L. MOODY

If there is any sin more deadly than envy,
it is being pleased at being envied.

RICHARD ARMOUR

The mind is its own place, and in itself can
make heaven of hell, a hell of heaven.

JOHN MILTON

Lord, make me an instrument of
your peace. Where there is hatred,
let me sow love; where there is injury,
pardon; where there is doubt, faith;
where there is despair, hope;
where there is darkness, light;
and where there is sadness, joy.

ST. FRANCIS OF ASSISI

The better part of one's life consists
of his friendships.

ABRAHAM LINCOLN

Friendship is one of the sweetest joys
of life. Many might have failed beneath
the bitterness of their trial, had they not
found a friend.

CHARLES SPURGEON

If, instead of a gem or even a flower,
we would cast the gift of a lovely thought
into the heart of a friend, that would be
giving as the angels give.

GEORGE MacDONALD

An ounce of wisdom is worth more
than tons of cleverness.

BALTASAR GRACIAN

If two friends ask you to judge a dispute,
don't accept, because you will lose one
friend; on the other hand, if two strangers
come with the same request, accept,
because you will gain one friend.

SAINT AUGUSTINE

In His plan for friends,
God often paints way
outside the lines.

Joy MacKenzie

For love is heaven, and heaven is love.

SIR WALTER SCOTT

All that is not eternal is out of date.

C.S. LEWIS

Happiness is a butterfly which when
pursued is just out of grasp... But if you
will sit down quietly, may alight upon you.

NATHANIEL HAWTHORNE

Happiness is the realization of God
in the heart. Happiness is the result
of praise and thanksgiving, of faith,
of acceptance; a quiet, tranquil
realization of the love of God.

WHITE EAGLE

First, keep peace within yourself;
then you can also bring peace to others.

THOMAS À KEMPIS

God go before you.
God stand behind you.
God watch above you.
Always, God love you.

LINDA BARNES

In the darkest part of the forest,
the spirit shines brightest.

LAUREN BENSON

I have been driven
many times to my knees
by the overwhelming
conviction that I had
nowhere else to go.

ABRAHAM LINCOLN

Mountaintops are for views and
inspiration, but fruit is grown
in the valleys.

BILLY GRAHAM

Trust God.
Sounds corny, works every time.

ELLEN BRENNEMAN

Work is not always required of a man.
There is such a thing as a sacred idleness,
the cultivation of which is now
fearfully neglected.

GEORGE MACDONALD

It is no use walking anywhere to preach,
unless our walking is our preaching.

ST. FRANCIS

God insists that we ask, not because He
needs to know our situation, but because
we need the spiritual discipline of asking.

CATHERINE MARSHALL

To be a Christian without prayer
is no more possible than to be alive
without breathing.

MARTIN LUTHER

If you can't hold your children in your arms,
please hold them in your hearts.

MOTHER CLARA HALE

What can you do to promote world peace?
Go home and love your family.

MOTHER TERESA

When God thought of mother,
he must have laughed with satisfaction
and framed it quickly – so rich, so deep,
so divine, so full of soul, power,
and beauty was the conception.

HENRY WARD BEECHER

Guided by my heritage of a love of beauty
and a respect for strength – in search of
my mother's garden I found my own.

ALICE WALKER

Two human loves make one divine.

ELIZABETH BARRETT BROWNING

The closer we are to God, the closer we are
to those who are close to him.

THOMAS MERTON

My dad will be the angel in heaven
who knows how to operate a miter saw.

JOHN PETERSON

So we could all have heroes,
God gave us dads.

GLENDA ALLEN

God loves each one of us
as if there were only one of us.

ST. AUGUSTINE

Every day we are called to small things
with great love.

MOTHER TERESA

You learn to speak by speaking,
To study by studying,
To run by running,
To work by working;
In just the same way you learn
to love by loving.

ST. FRANCIS DE SALES

Pray hard, work hard,
and leave the rest
to God.

FLORENCE GRIFFITH JOYNER,
OLYMPIC MEDALIST

God's promises are like the stars;
the darker the night,
the brighter they shine.

DAVID NICHOLAS

When we wake up in the morning
and turn our soul toward You,
You are there first.

SOREN KIERKEGAARD

Our God is an awesome God.

RICH MULLINS

No water's too deep
with God as your floaties.

AMY TROWBRIDGE-YATES

We recognize the nature of God best,
not by thinking about his power or wisdom,
which are terrifying, but by thinking about
his goodness and love. Then we are truly
born anew in God, and we can grow in faith.

MARTIN LUTHER

Love multiplies. It does not divide.

KRISTIN ARMSTRONG

Never forget that only dead fish
always swim with the stream.

MALCOLM MUGGERIDGE

The impulse of love that leads us to
the doorway of a friend is the voice
of God within, and we need
not be afraid to follow it.

AGNES SANFORD

Kind words are never wasted.
Like scattered seeds, they spring up
in unexpected places.

E. M. BOUNDS

Kind words can be short and easy to speak,
but their echoes are truly endless.

MOTHER TERESA

Few delights can equal the mere presence
of one whom we trust utterly.

GEORGE MACDONALD

Joy is the serious business of heaven.

C.S. LEWIS

If you judge people, you have no time
to love them.

MOTHER TERESA

God's goodness is spurred by His nature,
not by our worthiness.

MAX LUCADO

Go and preach the gospel.
Use words, if necessary.

ST. FRANCIS

And in the end, it's not the years in your life that count. It's the life in your years.

ABRAHAM LINCOLN

If you do not hope, you will not find what is beyond your hopes.

ST. CLEMENT OF ALEXANDRIA

Happiness is only in loving.

LEO TOLSTOY

Where your pleasure is,
there is your treasure.
Where your treasure is,
there is your heart.
Where your heart is,
there is your happiness.

St. Augustine

Happy is the day when I can
put a smile on someone's face.

Scott Degelman

Value not so much the gift of the lover
as the love of the giver.

Thomas à Kempis

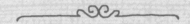

The more I wonder,
the more I love.

ALICE WALKER

Love liberates everything.

MAYA ANGELOU

The hunger for love is more difficult
to feed than the hunger for bread.

MOTHER TERESA

Duty takes us to places we never expected;
love brings us home.

SARAH MUELLER

It is in giving oneself that one receives.

ST. FRANCIS

Courage is fear that has said its prayers.

DOROTHY BERNARD

Hope is the power of being cheerful in
circumstances which we know
to be desperate.

G.K. CHESTERTON

What the world really needs is more love
and less paperwork.

PEARL BAILEY

God has a plan for all of us, but He expects
us to do our share of the work.

MINNIE PEARL

Doing what God requires is a sign of
superior wisdom. God requires that you
work hard at your calling without
worrying about what anyone else is doing.

MARTIN LUTHER

Whoever loves true life,
will love true love.

ELIZABETH BARRETT BROWNING

Love cannot be forced...
It comes out of Heaven,
unasked and unsought.

PEARL S. BUCK

TEN COMMANDMENTS FOR MOTHERS

Thou shalt drive the car pool
to the ends of the earth.

Thou shalt find the missing sock.

Thou shalt cut both pieces of cake
EXACTLY the same size.

Thou shalt NOT get sick when the kids do.

Thou shalt answer questions about
geography, long division,
and where babies come from.

Thou shalt walk slowly
and carry a big purse.

Thou shalt stop on the highway
to rescue the turtle...and give the kids
raw hot dogs to feed it.

Thou shalt smile through a zillion recitals
and ball games.

Thou shalt not admit thou art
related to – much less kiss – thine
adolescent in public.

Thou shalt give thyself time to
relax and enjoy life.

GINNIE JOB

The place God calls you to is the place
where your deep gladness and the world's
deep hunger meet.

FREDERICK BUECHNER

My mother told me I was blessed,
and I have always taken her word for it.
Being born of – or reincarnated from –
royalty is nothing like being blessed.
Royalty is inherited from another human
being; blessedness comes from God.

DUKE ELLINGTON

The woman is the heart of the home.

MOTHER TERESA

Someone who's obsessed with making money to the exclusion of other goals in life has likely forgone the possibility of the acceptance in God's kingdom.

JIMMY CARTER

No one is poor who has a godly mother.

ABRAHAM LINCOLN

A mother is she who can take the
place of all others, but whose place
no one else can take.

CARDINAL MERMILLOD

Women, if the soul of the nation
is to be saved, I believe that you must
become its soul.

CORETTA SCOTT KING

I know God will not give me anything
I can't handle. I just wish He didn't
trust me so much.

MOTHER TERESA

It's a good thing to have all the props
pulled out from under us occasionally.
It gives us some sense of what is rock
under our feet, and what is sand.

MADELEINE L'ENGLE

Troubles are often the tools by which
God fashions us for better things.

HENRY WARD BEECHER

God doesn't always
smooth the path,
but sometimes He puts
springs in the wagon.

MARSHALL LUCAS

When it rains on your parade,
look up rather than down. Without the
rain, there would be no rainbow.

G.K. CHESTERTON

We are not here to be successful.
We are here to be faithful.

MOTHER TERESA

Make each day your masterpiece.

JOHN WOODEN